3 1994 01098 7052

SANTA ANA PUBLIC LIBRARY

AR PTS: 0.5

D0572738

LETTERS HOME
from
ZIMBABWE

Lisa Halvorsen

J 916.891 HAL
Halvorsen, Lisa
Zimbabwe

JUN 2 9 2001 $16.95
CENTRAL   31994010987052

BLACKBIRCH PRESS, INC.

WOODBRIDGE, CONNECTICUT

Published by Blackbirch Press, Inc.
260 Amity Road
Woodbridge, CT 06525

©2000 by Blackbirch Press, Inc.
First Edition

e-mail: staff@blackbirch.com
Web site: www.blackbirch.com

All rights reserved. No part of this book may be reproduced in any form without permission in writing from Blackbirch Press, Inc., except by a reviewer.

Printed in Singapore

10 9 8 7 6 5 4 3 2 1

All photographs ©Corel Corporation, except pages 1 and 17: ©Corbis Corporation.

Library of Congress Cataloging-in-Publication Data
Halvorsen, Lisa.
Zimbabwe / by Lisa Halvorsen.
     p.   cm. — (Letters home from . . .)
Includes index.
ISBN 1-56711-412-1
1. Zimbabwe—Description and travel—Juvenile literature. 2. Halvorsen, Lisa—Journeys—Zimbabwe—Juvenile literature. [1. Zimbabwe—Description and travel.]
I. Title. II. Series.
DT2904.H35   2000
916.89104'51—dc21
                                                      00-009385

TABLE OF CONTENTS

Arrival in . . .

Harare

We just landed in Harare, the capital of Zimbabwe. I read about the wildlife and interesting sights of this African country on the plane. Now I can't wait to start exploring its national parks, cities, and natural wonders.

Zimbabwe is a landlocked country in south-central Africa. It was known as Southern Rhodesia until 1980. That's when it gained independence from Great Britain and changed its name. Its neighbors are Zambia, Namibia, Botswana, South Africa, and Mozambique.

Although Zimbabwe is located in the tropics, much of the country is on a high plateau. So it's not as hot as you might expect. It's about 151,000 square miles in size. That's slightly larger than Montana. More than 11 million people live here.

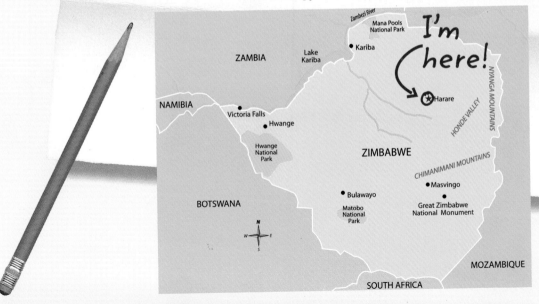

Harare

Harare, the Sunshine City, is much larger and more modern than I imagined. This morning we walked through African Unity Square on our way to visit the Parliament Building. Before independence, this was known as Cecil Square. Cecil Rhodes founded the city in 1890. He called it Fort Salisbury. Rhodes was British and made his fortune mining diamonds in South Africa. He and others settled in what is now Zimbabwe.

Later we wandered through the Mbare Musika (market). It was crowded and noisy. The local people come here to buy everything from woven baskets to live chickens. Then we drove to the top of The Kopje for a good view of the city.

Sugar cane and fruit

Plants and Trees

We learned a lot about Zimbabwe's plants and trees at the National Botanical Gardens just outside the city center. These gardens contain most of its 750 native species of trees. One of the most unusual is the sausage tree. It gets its name from its big, brown, sausage-shaped fruits. These fruits can grow more than 3 feet long! Medical researchers think a paste made from the dried fruit may someday be used to cure some skin cancers.

The baobab tree, with its rootlike branches, looks like it was planted upside down! We also saw acacia trees, a favorite food of elephants, and lots of aloe trees. Many other species—like the jacaranda and bauhinia—have beautiful flowers.

Baobab tree

Aloe trees

Honde Valley

This morning we headed out of the city towards the Eastern Highlands. This part of Zimbabwe has the coolest temperatures and the most rainfall. As we passed through a small village in the Honde Valley south of Harare, I spotted some round huts with thatched roofs.

The Shona people live in these huts, which are called rondavels. About 71% of Zimbabweans are Shonas. About 16% are Ndebele. Although English is the official language of the country, Chishona and Sindebele are also widely spoken.

Honde Valley community

Bus in Honde Valley

Tea plantations

Rondavels

The Honde Valley is located at the foot of the Nyanga mountain range, which joins Mozambique. It is very hot and humid here. This makes it a great place to grow tropical fruits. There are also many tea and coffee plantations.

Agriculture is an important industry throughout the country, not just in this river valley. The main crops are maize (corn), cotton, tobacco, wheat, sugarcane, coffee, and peanuts. Many farmers raise cattle, sheep, goats, and pigs. Some even have ostrich farms.

Chimanimani Mountains

Today we traveled to the rugged Chimanimani Mountains. They are the biggest mountain range in the country. They are located at the southern end of the Eastern Highlands and are part of the 42,200-acre Chimanimani National Park. Binga, the tallest peak in this range, is 8,003 feet above sea level. Many people come to the highlands to escape the heat. The vegetation is different here. You can find heather, mountain hibiscus, ferns, and orchids. It's a good place to study rare plant species or go birdwatching. Some of the birds here have really unusual names like purple-crested lourie, trumpeter hornbill, and secretary bird.

Chimanimani Mountains

Purple-crested lourie

Chimanimani Mountains

Road to Chimanimani Mountains

According to my guidebook, the Chimanimanis are one of 3 mountain ranges that make up the highlands. The Nyanga Mountains are in the north. Zimbabwe's highest peak, 8,504-foot Mount Inyangani, is part of this range. The middle range is the Bvumba.

If you are lucky, you might spot a sable antelope, bushbuck, eland, or the rare blue duiker. These are all African antelopes. Or maybe you'll see a samango monkey. This is one of the few places in Africa where they're found. Leopards also live in these mountains but are rarely seen.

Great Zimbabwe National Monument

We arrived in Masvingo last night. This mining and farming community was the first white settlement in Zimbabwe. It was originally named Fort Victoria. It's a good place to stay to visit the Great Zimbabwe National Monument. These 13th-century stone ruins are just 17 miles southeast of town.

Our guide explained that Zimbabwe comes from "mazimbabwe." That's a Shona word for "houses of stone." He said that Adam Renders, a German hunter, was the first European to see these ruins in 1867.

Great Enclosure

Aloe trees by the wall

The wall, Great Zimbabwe National Monument

Conical tower

Chinese porcelain, glass beads, gold ornaments, and other artifacts discovered at the site indicate that this was an early center of trading. The walls and structures were built between A.D. 950 and 1450 by ancestors of today's Zimbabweans.

There are 3 main walled complexes on almost 1,800 acres. The most awesome was the Great Enclosure. It is 36 feet high and more than 800 feet around. Our guide said it probably surrounded the houses and buildings of the royal family. He also said that no mortar or mud was used to hold the stones together!

Matobo National Park

We are now in Matobo National Park in western Zimbabwe. This park is about 25 miles south of Bulawayo, the second-largest city in Zimbabwe. Its terrain is very hilly with lots of big boulders.

The Ndebele king Mzilikazi named these hills "Amatobo." It means "bald-headed ones." I think this is a good description of the round, treeless, granite hills. Later, white settlers changed the name to Matobo. One third of the world's 47 eagle species nest here. This is also where you will find the largest concentration of black eagles on the planet! They feed on a furry, short-legged animal called a hyrax (rock rabbit).

Buying crafts at the market, Matobo

Matobo National Park

Rock design

Rhode's grave, "World's View"

Our guide called this the world's largest rock-art gallery! Most of the more than 2,000 rock paintings in Zimbabwe are found in caves here. Many are of animals, including kudus, giraffes, and white rhinoceroses. They were painted with pigment made from plants, animal fat, and blood. Researchers believe the San people, who were hunter-gathers, did these paintings. They lived in this area 6,000 to 10,000 years ago! Some of the best-preserved paintings are found in Nswatugi Cave in this park.

Matobo is a sacred area for the Ndebele people. Cecil Rhodes also considered this to be a special place. He asked to be buried on top of one of the hills. We hiked up the path to see "World's View," Rhodes' burial place, before we headed back to Bulawayo.

Hwange National Park

I'm so excited! This morning we arrived in Hwange where we will head out on our first wildlife safari! Hwange is a community of about 40,000 people in northwestern Zimbabwe. Its main industry is coal although copper and tin mines were opened here recently. Zimbabwe is a mineral-rich country. It has significant deposits of coal, chromium ore, gold, nickel, silver, and iron, among other mineral resources.

To the south is Zimbabwe's largest game park, Hwange National Park. The 5,000-square-mile park is located along the Botswana border. Its central and southern regions form the northeastern tip of the Kalahari Desert. Vast sections are covered with sand, sparse grass, and dry scrub-land.

Elephant crossing

Road sign

Hwange National Park

Impala

In the 1800s, this was a hunting reserve for Ndebele kings. Today it is one of only a few elephant sanctuaries in Africa. The game warden told us that herds of up to 100 elephants often drink at the water holes.

From our safari vehicle we spotted impalas, zebras, giraffes, baboons, jackals, and even a pride of lions. We got so close to the animals that I didn't even need to use my binoculars! Our guide explained that these are just a few of the 105 species of animals and 400 species of birds here. It's also the only protected area with large groups of gemsbok (oryx) and brown hyena. Hwange's wild dog population is the biggest in all of Africa.

Wildlife

Hwange is just one of 16 national parks in the country. There are also many conservation areas and game reserves. About 11% of the land has been set aside by the government to protect native animals and conserve the natural landscape.

The 5 best-known African wild animals live in Zimbabwe—the lion, leopard, elephant, buffalo, and rhinoceros. The biggest is the African elephant. In fact, we learned that it is the largest land mammal on Earth.

Cape buffalo

Zebra with oxpecker

Warthog

Giraffes

I took lots of photos of elephants, the long-necked giraffes, and warthogs. The warthog is a funny-looking wild pig with warts on its face and curving tusks. Our guide said that the best time to view wild game is in the cooler parts of the day—dawn and dusk. That's when they are most active. They rest when it is hot.

Our guide pointed out that many birds depend on animals for their food. The oxpecker gets a free ride on the zebra's back. It picks off ticks that hop on the zebra as it walks through the grassland.

Victoria Falls

Today we saw the largest waterfalls in the world! They are twice as tall as Niagara Falls. Water has been flowing over them for more than 2 million years! They are located on the Zambezi River, 621 miles from its source in northwestern Zambia.

The falls are 1.5 miles wide. At their deepest point, they drop 355 feet into the Zambezi Gorge. The roar of the rushing waters is so loud that you can hear it 25 miles away!

Victoria Falls

Victoria Falls

Mist over
Victoria Falls

Victoria Falls

I read in my guidebook that Scottish missionary-explorer David Livingstone was the first European to see the falls. The year was 1855. He named them for Queen Victoria of England. The Kololo tribe who lived nearby at that time called them Mosi-oa-Tunya, "the smoke that thunders."

A statue of Livingstone stands overlooking Devil's Cataract. This is the lowest of 5 separate falls that make up Victoria Falls. The others are Horseshoe Falls, Main Falls, Rainbow Falls, and Eastern Cataract.

Although a few people traveled to see the falls in the late 1800s, it wasn't until 1905 that the real tourist boom started. That's when Cecil Rhodes extended his railway north. Today the falls are Zimbabwe's most popular tourist destination.

Zambezi River

People come to view the falls but also to go white-water rafting on the fast-flowing Zambezi River. Some even bungee jump off the railway bridge that crosses over the river to Zambia. The Victoria Falls Bridge was built in 1905. Rhodes wanted the train passengers to feel the spray of the falls on their faces. So he had the bridge built very close to the falls.

It was originally designed for sets of train tracks. Now cars and trucks, as well as trains, pass over it. You can walk across it, too. We did, and we got soaked, even though we were wearing raincoats!

Landscape along Zambezi River

Zambezi River

Victoria Falls Hotel

Later, we took the Flight of Angels over the falls. From the plane window I snapped tons of photos of the falls, the mighty Zambezi, and the river gorges. I also saw a double rainbow shining in the mist. It was awesome!

We stayed at the elegant Victoria Falls Hotel. The original hotel was built of wood with a corrugated tin roof at the turn of the last century. After supper, we headed to the forest of ebony, fig, and mahogany trees on the edge of the falls. This forest is home to a rare fern found in only two other places in the world. On our walk we startled a group of vervet monkeys who quickly darted away from us into the underbrush.

Artisans and Crafts

At the falls we saw many people selling crafts. This is a good way for them to make extra money to support their families. Throughout our travels we have seen many handmade crafts for sale by the side of the road or at local markets.

We stopped to watch some women who were crocheting. I was amazed at how fast they worked. For most women this is not a full-time job, but something they do in their spare time. In traditional Zimbabwean families, women take care of the home and children. They also cook, clean, and help with the plowing, planting, and harvesting of crops.

Potter at work

Women doing crochet work

Craft market, Birchenoff Bridge

Wooden mask

In some rural areas, women's craft cooperatives have been set up by missions and non-government organizations. Through these cooperatives women learn how to make and market crafts like baskets, pottery, batik, and crocheted clothing. They may meet together a few times a week to work on their crafts.

Men also make things to sell. Some make carved wooden masks. Others make soapstone sculptures. Soapstone is a soft black or brown rock found throughout the country. The men carve birds, animals, and human figures out of the stone using a hammer and chisel.

25

Lake Kariba

We took the river ferry from Mlibisi near Victoria Falls to Kariba. It took us almost a day. But believe it or not, it was still quicker than traveling 750 miles by road! Going by water was a lot of fun! We drifted by crocodiles sleeping on river banks and hippopotamuses submerged up to their eyeballs in the muddy water. We also saw birds called weavers busy at work building hanging nests in trees.

A crew member told us that the Zambezi River forms a natural border between Zimbabwe and Zambia. It is Africa's fourth-largest river. He said it is 1,650 miles from its source in northwestern Zambia to its mouth on the Indian Ocean.

Weaver nests, near Zambezi River

Tree skeleton near Kariba

Sunset, Lake Kariba

Hydroelectric dam

Early traders used the river to ship gold, ivory, and slaves from Africa's interior to the coast. Livingstone tried to navigate its length by steamer, but gave up when he couldn't get past one of the gorges.

The river was dammed in the late 1950s to provide hydroelectric power to Zambia and Zimbabwe. When it was built, it was the largest dam in the world! Before it could be started, the local Batonga tribe—who lived on the floodplain—had to be moved to a new home.

Lake Kariba was formed when the river was dammed. You can see dead trees and stumps sticking out of the water. The lake is 175 miles long and 20 miles wide. It is Africa's third-largest lake.

Fothergill Island

We stayed overnight in a thatched roof lodge on Fothergill Island in Lake Kariba. It was named for Rupert Fothergill. This game warden led one of the greatest wildlife rescue missions ever. In Operation Noah, he and other volunteers tracked, captured, and moved 5,000 animals, including rhinoceroses and lions, to save them from the rising waters when the dam was built.

We saw some termite mounds as well. They are made from a mixture of termite saliva and bits of dirt. That's where the termites live. Some mounds can be as tall as 20 feet!

Termite mound

Fothergill

Elephants feeding, Fothergill

Safari camp

Staying on Fothergill Island was fun, especially because we got to go fishing for tiger fish! These freshwater fish have a striped body and big teeth—just like a tiger! They also fight hard when you try to reel them in. The biggest tiger fish ever caught here weighed 34 pounds! While we were fishing, we had to keep an eye out for crocodiles.

Other fish species—like the capenta and Tanganyika sardine—were released into the lake. The sardine was brought in from Lake Tanganyika. That lake forms a boundary between the Democratic Republic of the Congo and Tanzania in east-central Africa. Both species are fished commercially. The fishing industry adds millions of dollars to the country's economy. It also provides jobs for 2,000 people!

Mana Pools National Park

We made one last stop before heading back to Harare for our flight home. We went to Mana Pools National Park in northeastern Zimbabwe. This 542,000-acre park gets its name from the pools carved out by the Zambezi River many years ago. When the river shifted its course, these pools remained and filled with water.

This is the only park in Zimbabwe where you are allowed to walk through the bush without a guide. Near park headquarters in Nyamepi we saw an elephant stand on its hind legs and use its trunk to pull fruit off an acacia tree. We also watched buffalos, kudus, elands, waterbucks, and zebras come to the pools to drink.

Cape buffalo

Carmine bee eater

Yellow-billed hornbill

Hippos in morning light

The game warden said that this park has the biggest population of hippopotamuses and crocodiles in all of Zimbabwe. There are also 350 species of birds, including the yellow-billed hornbill. Some, like the fish eagle, African skimmer, and carmine bee eater, are rare in other parts of Africa but common at Mana Pools.

This area was once home to the largest black rhinoceros population in the world. But poachers killed many of this endangered species. Today, not many are left. But wildlife experts are working hard to protect the remaining animals and increase their numbers in the wild.

31

Glossary

Batik cloth decorated by a method of dyeing designs on cloth by coating the parts that aren't to be dyed with wax.

Cooperative an organization set up for the production or marketing of goods that is owned and operated for the benefit of its members.

Kopje an African word for small hill.

Kudu an African antelope.

Mortar a mixture of cement or sand and water used between stones to hold them together.

Poachers people who take game animals or fish illegally.

Pride a group or family of lions.

Safari a Swahili word for journey.

Thatch a roof made of straw, palm leaves, or other plant materials.

Veld African grassland or open grassy country with few bushes and trees.

For More Information

Books

Barnes-Svarney, Patricia L. *Zimbabwe* (Major World Nations). New York, NY: Chelsea House, 1997.

Bessire, Mark. *Great Zimbabwe* (African Civilizations). Danbury, CT: Franklin Watts, Inc., 1999.

Dudley, Karen. *Elephants* (Untamed World). Chatham, NJ: Raintree/Steck Vaughn, 1997.

Regan, Colm. Pedar Cremin. *Africa* (Continents). Chatham, NJ: Raintree/Steck Vaughn, 1997.

Web Site
Mbira

Learn about Zimbabwe's culture, including its music and customs—www.tiac.net/users/smurungu/home.html.

Index